waking the wild

Nadia Hasan

a poetry collection

Waking the Wild
Copyright © 2016 by Nadia Hasan.
All rights reserved.

Printed in the United States of America. No part of this book may be used or reproduced whatsoever without written permission except in the case of reprints in the context of reviews.

Please note the scanning, uploading, and distributing of this book via the internet or other means without prior written consent of the copyright owner is illegal and punishable by law. Please purchase only authorized electronic editions, and do not participate in or encourage electronic piracy of copyrighted materials.

Edited by Dionne Lister
Cover design by Najla Qamber Designs www.najlaqamberdesigns.com
Book design by Nadège Richards of Inkstain Interior Book Design

THIS BOOK IS DEDICATED TO:

Nathaniel—
Your imagination, wonder and kindness are things that I will always miss. You had a way of looking at the world around you that was truly magical.

Kianna—
My Twin, my Ride-or-Die, my best friend, I am so much more for having known you and so much less now that you are gone. I love you.

& Sherry (Mom)—
I will always be grateful to you for raising two beautiful, unique, caring souls who forever changed my life and blessed it immeasurably. Thank you.

CONTENTS

Traveler | 1
Staged | 3
Traces | 5
Night Mary | 7
Composure | 9
Footnotes | 11
Genesis | 13
Appetites | 15
Connections | 17
Counsel | 19
Lighthouse | 21
Little Things | 23
When You're Far Away | 25
I Hope You Know | 27
Control | 29
Unbroken Bonds | 31
Persephone's Last | 33
Accelerant | 35
La Vida Lotus | 37
Waking the Wild | 39
Humanity | 41
Familiar | 43

All Souls | 45
Whirlpool | 47
The Waiting | 49
Leaving a Light On | 51
Clarity | 53
When You Wanted… | 55
Circumstances | 57
Unwell | 59
From 11:22 | 61
No Words | 63
Decipher | 65
Vigil | 67
Unsent Letter #1 | 69
What I Cannot Bring Myself to Say | 71
Ellipsis | 75
Why Do I Keep Doing This? | 77
When the Body Betrays | 79
Thoughts at Your Funeral | 81
Error | 83
Discontent | 85
I Will Be | 87
There Will Be a Day | 89
Whenever | 91

waking the wild

traveler

Can your soul hear
the call of the sun
beckoning your return?

Do the mountains
echo through a
misty shroud of memories

and the spirits of your
ancestors sing from
beneath the earth?

Can you feel the pull
of a far-off place

that you have never seen

but find nightly in
dreams that you can't
quite recall?

A land that you've never
tread, never lived in and
yet, never left at all.

staged

Fine.
What a lie.
Said so much
like it's a line
in a rehearsed play.
Why do we bite back
all the things
we want to say?
Why
do we put up brave fronts
when we're so far
from okay?

Traces

My hair is constantly shedding
leaving strands woven into clothes or
wrapped around fingers,
falling into carpets.

Maybe my DNA is careless
or carefree
A friend says losing hair
is natural, we lose so many strands a day.

Another friend plucks my strands
from between her fingers, twisting it

"I'll save it for voodoo or something."
and she smiles.

Maybe it's a gift
traces of myself that I'll leave
behind, when people often disappear so quickly
leaving nothing at all.
I can't help wondering
what other pieces of myself have I lost,
walked away from,
without realizing they were gone?

Night Mary

She loved to consume darkness
like blackberries
that stained her mouth and hands

she was insatiable

she would revel in it,
cutting shadows for her clothing
dancing with midnight
painting moonlight on her eyelids -

but she would never lay within it

Nadia Hasan

dark rooms, she said,
were too much like caskets
and sleeping in them
was far too much

like being buried alive.

Composure

Serendipity wrote a serenade
just for them
leading them away and back like
a fairy tale, but only stories
have happy endings

they were pulled together as taut as
a violin string

the collision like
rumbling bass at a
heavy metal concert

Straight to the heart
and through bone

they were shaken

dizzy, delirious in the crescendo
they composed symphonies
of passages inbetween

lullabies that led them to love,
like constellations burning in
the darkness of night

Then

their parting was a sonata,
a melancholy melody
that left no notes
to its goodbye.

Footnotes

You made your choice
didn't look back
so what gives you the right
to return to my pages
now?

Genesis

we grew together
from saplings to intertwining
vines, and the growing pains were
tremendous,
but we survived

and you are best friend,
sister, semblance of so much in
each other
that we reflect, we refract, we collide sometimes
but we survive

and you are nearer and dearer to me
than a shadow. we lose touch

but never grow apart,
these hearts are kindred

and I can grieve for you when
you need to be strong
and I cry for you, break for you,
when you need to stay together
and life is hard sometimes
but we'll survive

just like we always have,
just like it always was,
two pillars in this dark tempest,
keeping each other strong

Appetites

If self-loathing were edible,
I'd never go hungry

no matter how hard I try
it's impossible to deny
that some days it's too hard
to not cry and stay positive.

Instead I feign confidence,
the most appealing component
in a well-balanced personality.

So every day I force feed
myself affirmations and practice

smiles, pushing down the bile
of bitterness and lie.

I won't think *I wish I was pretty*
every time I see my reflection, pleading
like a hail Mary for vindication
from imperfection.

I will do better today,
and when you hand me
compliments, I won't reveal
how difficult they are for me
to digest.

Connections

How do I
answer such a simple question
knowing you'll never understand
my answer?

I wish it were simple
but our relationship has always
been anything but.

Even now I can feel the pull
of our connection
that I both love and hate

whose sway I thought
was long since buried
since I alone
find it significant.

Counsel

I walked from a wintry forest filled with light
to a field engulfed in summer's night,
the cicadas were calling
and there was a lone caravan
with the door thrown open
wide

I heard the call through beaded curtain,
murmuring softly, *come inside*

so I went through the veil
and sat at a table where
a triple moon's light danced

on its mahogany surface,
the milky glow matching
the old woman's eyes

Why have you come?

I could not answer
I didn't know
but she tapped her temple
and tossed down three cards,
all blank

I leaned forward, frowned

You're looking in the wrong places.

she tapped my arms,
where all the words I had for you
some secret, some unknown, some acknowledged
were written in red clay

She said, *you already have the answers.*
You are only afraid to ask the right questions.

Lighthouse

There should have been a warning label:
Handle With Care
but there was none and people are so careless.
the sea was a beckoning friend
so endless.

The pitch of the song in her soul
could have been
a wailing siren, screaming
for all the world to hear.

But only two things exist:
the right ones and
the wrong ones.

It wasn't a cry for help.
 It was her battle cry, a cry for hope
and sometimes, an echo of
defeat.

She was a storm, battered against a perilous
coast, where she returned
again and again.

She couldn't be tamed,
yet they still tried to break her.
They love you best
when you are broken.

She built up her walls, dimmed her lights,
became a ghost haunting the night.
The right ones waited,
knowing only patience.

Shh, be still.

They were content to wait
sitting by her side, convinced that
she would live again.
She was still strong, and after some time
she took a deep breath,
and shined.

(10W*)

Little Things

Time
is evanescent
I won't regret
saying
I Love You

*10W is an abbreviation for ten word, a short-form poetry style, which originated on *Hello Poetry*.

When You're Far Away

You must be tired
of hearing me say
I miss you

so instead
I'll tell you
how amazing you are

all the things I love
about you

all of the traits
I admire

and recount
all the times
you've made me smile

and brought light
the way only you can
into my life
which is so often dark
and difficult

(10+2)

I Hope You Know

This has **never** been easy
but you have always been
worth it.

Control

She blooms at night
like jasmine
in darkness, slowly,

the perfume of longing
is strong, stirring inside her,
foreign and secret.

In daylight she pretends
she is merely a little girl playing
dress up, naïve and uncomplicated
the way she knows you

love her best

though she is somewhere
inbetween everything
she always was and could yet be.

You fill her with shame
at the brightness of her petals,
in fear and dread of the day
she might outgrow the garden
you planted her in.

You call her a weed, in a
pathetic ploy for control
knowing she is far more

like a fire
waiting to burn free,
you try and temper
her glow.

Unbroken Bonds

She asked, what if
we come back and repeat
everything over again,

and we would keep going
until everything is just
right?

If we could, I think
I would cherish you
even more each time

and be just as fond of
the wonderful memories
I have made here.

I wouldn't have this
life any other way,
and any one without you
wouldn't do at all.

Persephone's Last

I'm wandering through fields
of wheat as he stalks me
through the grain

I cannot see him but I
know he's there, the king
of death and frost

he's an omen to the living
and a comfort to the lost
a cloak of night hides his face,
but it's always the same

a calling
a longing
for my company
an end to eternal pain

the sun is strong, clings to my
skin, and a crow circles
overhead

preparing my soul to alight
to the kingdom
of the dead

he's at my heels and I
try to fight but he pushes me
through the dirt

his breath embalms me
cold as ice, he whispers

"hush my love, my dear one,
I promise this won't hurt."

Accelerant

She couldn't blame him
completely
No, she placed blame in the hands of people
who failed to protect them
who sacrificed their innocence
to monsters who wore guises of man.

Hungrily feasting
on any light that grew vulnerable
they left holes in young hearts.

Dimmed the hope,
so that doubt and dark
reverberated in the chasms
left behind.

Nadia Hasan

Spaces
so wide
that anguish created
its own echo.

Emptying bottles like it held a message,
maybe some directions
to where it all went wrong,
or answers to what was
wrong inside them.

Drinking, thinking
that it can erase the pain,
kill the beast,
fill the longing.

Too lost to know
that this is not a cure
but a curse,
killing the last vestiges of self
from the inside

giving the darkness
somewhere to grow.

La Vida Lotus

Beautiful things grow
out of bad situations
shitty conditions
at rock bottom
or in seconds chances

Don't ever
let Them tell you
you are
too broken
to bloom

waking the wild

Lilac and lavender dance at her hem,
bare feet soothe traces in the earth,
onyx contrasts to emerald green-
the blades blink away sleep

a hushed horizon disperses robin's-egg blue
Hello, Morning!
dressed in drops of silver dew

the breeze gently threads
golden, watercolor sunrise
into her hair as she closes her eyes

Nadia Hasan

her open arms plead,
haunted and hungry

his skin, smelling of comfrey
musk and mystery
as clove and rose linger
like confessions
on his lips

Humanity

There is a defect in us
as human beings
because we think ourselves
a fortress, a mountain, unbreakable
but at the center
in that stillness of being
there is a chasm
of love
which echoes hope, compassion, empathy
try again, it says
and though the fault lines are full of darkness
we are held together by
the optimism and foolishness
of a single spark

Familiar

Some days
I will think I see you
on crowded streets
in busy malls
on rides in festivals and fairgrounds
and I will think of you
in every child that passes by
in every sound of laughter,
through every tear at four a.m.
because
I still dream about
things that could've been:
you stealing my toys
then my clothes

Nadia Hasan

all the stupid fights
and
family photos
vacations
days of homework
school dances
that never were

How we could all
be together
in another life
if things were different,
But instead
I
hold onto
loving you
even though we may never meet
and I can never forget
your faces

All Souls

We're all just holding on
looking for something to burn
away
the cold loneliness in the darkness
we cling to our lies
make up faces that stare back
strangers

We're all just ghosts
wanting to feel and be felt
we dream of that one
(you know the one)

Nadia Hasan

in our sleep, clutching their echoes
endlessly
reaching out

whirlpool

Debris of the day settles
in her stomach like sand,
grit lining the bottom of the ocean
like pollution, plastic rings cutting
into organs, thoughts drifting useless,
memories like broken bits of wine bottles
skimming the floor:

Shallow and deep, rolling
waves, riptides
why doesn't he think I'm
pretty, please don't let me keep
remembering the weight of her arms
peaceful, still, unbroken heart

holding her until the screams start
and she follows...

And she falls apart...
no more laughter, no more intact
hearts only empty arms
and half-assed, hopeful, loving

Good.

Am I good? Is this
good?

Is this living?

The Waiting

Four hundred thousand five hundred forty children
Waiting for forever families
for happy homes
Safety.

Acceptance,
a place of their own
where they can stay
to be loved, in permanent ink
to fit,
or fill that empty space.

Trying to forget
or remember,
who they are
what they've lost
and Why.

Why?

Questioning
All the reasons, they were left behind,
taken away,
Forgotten.

Like discarded furniture
after people have moved on.

Leaving a Light On

These thoughts
leave me lingering
on the back porch of hope,

where it's housed,
warm and unfamiliar,
calling for me to come
and leave my armor
at its doorstep.

Doubt and Pessimism
are unrelenting weeds that
grow everywhere in the backyard

of self-esteem,

they are familiar and welcoming
and have convinced me
that I can live just as comfortably
there.

So I sit,
undecidedly afraid
that disappointment may fall
as sure as night,

and in the darkness
of indecision, Hope
flips on a light.

clarity

In silence
as you let your thoughts
wander, things will fall
into place

Maybe the reason that
you don't believe Them
for whatever reason
is because
you're used to
being disrespected
and somehow

Nadia Hasan

like a ripple on the surface
everything is not as still
inside you.

When
did you start
telling yourself
this was
okay?

when you wanted...

I tried to find the words
when you wanted a voice
but I suspect, any would do

You never could appreciate
who I was or what I had to give
I think, we all looked like
whatever you needed us to

Maybe carbon copies
of the one you wanted
when you wanted to be loved

I wanted that, too.

Circumstances

Truth be told
we all doubt one another
Between what is said
and what sits in a heart

All these years
I have yet to discover
what holds some people
or keeps others apart

Unwell

Muscles throb and ache
asleep or wide awake
10mg, 800mg, heating pad
tolerance tango.

What may work today
might fail miserably tomorrow.

Consecutive days of pain,
but I want to be strong
in your eyes.

Nadia Hasan

Don't ask how I am,
you deserve better
than lies.

From 11:22

Night is
a dove cradled
in an inkwell
whose flight carries inspiration
on its wings

No Words

I cannot think
I cannot breathe
This
isn't happening

Remember it all or
numb it away
My backbone
my other half
my Twin

Justice and Vengeance
Night and Day
The other half to this broken heart

Nadia Hasan

I need you to fight
I need you to stay

I am crumbling breaking
Please, don't
leave me
Without you
I can't do it alone

You know
I was never that strong

Decipher

I am so much less without you
So much worse, incomplete
unraveling
The emotions pour out of this black hole space where
my heart used to be
sucking my breath
the grief pinging off my ribcage like pebbles off a
windshield
I am cracked
I am broken
and all my words come out wrong but
there are no words
and nothing matters

Nadia Hasan

My own body exhausts me
I collapse in on myself
I hear the fireworks
Loud cracks and booms
and I think:
Maybe the world has fallen apart.
I don't care.
You are the only one who can
make sense of anything
or love me
or forgive me
Don't leave me
I need you

Vigil

We sit in silence
our shared misery
spread between us like continents

What a mess you have left,
frayed friendships and messy entanglements
a love only just beginning
all plans and dreams

Brought to a standstill

Our only familiar ground is

our love for you, our hope for you
to pull through

We hold each other upright
grasp tightly to shoulders,
our bodies bent over the yawning caverns
of despair, afraid that acknowledging the reality
will cause us to stumble, and swallow us whole

Life has become a little difficult to stomach
and we've become the ghosts,

barely eating, barely breathing
our eyes haunt doorways and window frames
expecting to see you, to hear you

We'll forgive this cruel deception
if only you come home again

Unsent Letter #1

Be here
accept
move forward
all that I am asked to do

Yet I struggle
when inside my bones,
deep in my marrow
emptiness exists like cavernous rooms
each one whispering your name,
overlapping, like prayer or invocation
to keep you alive
or bring you back

Nadia Hasan

Those who love you
carry a unique pain,
no one else can comprehend because
to love you and to be loved by you
is the kind of gift
so many search for and
we were lucky to ever obtain
even once

What I Cannot Bring Myself To Say

1.
Pity for the poor man
for the rabid monster
for the lonely lost boy you must have been
What did you let nest in your empty spaces,
which in turns speaks to you to recreate them in others?

It isn't okay
and I haven't begun to forgive you

2.
He tells me he wasn't thinking,
letting his words fall from his mouth like discarded
clothing-
and only now realized the smell

I think of other hands that were just as careless, blindly

swinging,
of words so sharp they cut,
leaving my mother to bleed alone, clumsy only in their botched attempt to kill-
and how she slowly began to clean.

Is it any wonder that I was born bearing the weight of a compulsion to fix
my birth like a thread that failed to stitch not one,
but two, broken people back together-

I am standing in the ruins of something that was beautiful
with the memory of my almost-not quite-step-father's careless anger
staring at the ruins of a boy who was beautiful, a lost lonely man-child,
who sits at the bottoms of bottles like a genie-
wishing them both full again.

Pity for the poor boys who climb the spines of women,
who seek solace in their wombs,
completion in the mind-body disconnect
of the evanescent orgasm

Pity for misguided girls, falsely believing
that giving them their hearts to stand on will make

them into men,
instead of taller boys.

It isn't okay, I tell him, but I forgive you.

3.
I am afraid that I will forever seek the storm.
I am compelled to fix. To stand in the downpour of his pain and brokenness,
not realizing it won't spare him-
it will continue to come long after I have drowned

I am afraid that I will not recognize love when it finds me.
that when this man arrives, I will distrust his gentle hand on my shoulder
I will seek to fix things that aren't broken,
haunted by the ruins of once beautiful things

that when he gently tells me to lay down my hammer,
which I so often avoid swinging at anyone but myself,
I will not know how to take leave of my mistrust and believe that he would simply be content to take my vacant hand and heart, and let us walk through life as equals-
to let something beautiful bloom in a poisoned bed

I hope then that I have the courage to grow. I hope that even as I struggle or misstep,
I tell myself:

It's okay, and I forgive you.

Ellipsis

I woke up this morning
feeling like my days had blurred
into a unending procession of sameness.

I wanted to call you
and talk about things
the way we used to do.

It's like we've become strangers
and my mourning makes it easy
to stop reaching out.

Nadia Hasan

I wanted to tell you that I love you
but I'm constricted by this feeling
that I don't know how to shake.

Our conversations repeat,
and I feel like I'm saying goodbye
to something that's already gone.

Don't you despise the way
everything we say to each other
ends unfinished or in question marks?

Why Do I Keep Doing This?

We used to lament for hours on why
we held on to those people we loved,
who didn't love us back, or didn't
love us enough or maybe didn't love us
the way we kept loving them. "Why
do I keep doing this?"

Is it fate or force?

It takes a lot to love someone that way. We kept
asking, "Would they care if I were to walk away?"
The problem was that every time we tried, suddenly
they'd appear without coercion, saying or doing what
we had
wished for in the first place. We'd commiserate, "Is it
supposed to

be this hard?" Neither of us held the answers, because you and I
loved in the same way. Selflessly, maddeningly, in ink and paper…
We secret romantics. I suppose that's why we're best friends.

Is it fate or force?

Now you're gone, and I question everything.
I question fate and whether we were ever meant to find our answers. Without the counterbalance of your logic, I distrust everything, even myself. "Is it supposed to
be this hard?" Because every day without you is difficult.
The answers seem trivial, but I keep asking myself the same questions.

Is it fate or force?

when the Body Betrays

If ever I'm in need of a reminder of what a survivor is
I should look no further than my own body

these bones are broken, battered, twisted markers of
just how badly I have fought to live, these scars are
a record of what I have sacrificed to overcome

and because the battle has been brutal, maybe
I should forgive myself for how imperfect, how
unbeautiful this body truly is

but you should not see me like this.

Nadia Hasan

Dear loved one, on the days when my body betrays itself
I do not wish you near me. I do not wish to be cared for when my muscles
are landmines, set to go off at any minute, the spasms squeezing me until
I can't breathe

my limbs, stiff and immobile, will crack
and I will cry, scream, fight, just to move an inch
any dignity will be lost and any strength will dissipate

Loved One, it will tear you down. Exhaust you. It will make you weary and angry,
and there will be days of this without end, without a solution.

How can you possibly love me then? If I truly loved you, then how could I ask you to?
How could I ask you to give up a life where struggle like this doesn't exist?

On days when my body betrays itself, I am not a warrior. I am not a fighter. I am simply a selfish being, at the mercy of her own pain, without hope that I can go on like this or that there's a future in which you would stay.

Thoughts at Your Funeral

You always told me
that funerals weren't for the person who died,
they were for the people that they left behind.

You said you refused to go to one ever, even your own,
so while I was at your funeral it was easy to believe
you weren't really gone.

On the day of your funeral
there was a rock concert going on
and I was convinced you were actually there instead.

But I also kept seeing you sitting next to me,

making sassy comments and faces during your eulogy,
and it was almost impossible not to laugh at how
ridiculous the whole thing was.

You told me that there were better ways to remember a person
and when you died I kept thinking
about all of the things you'd want me to do.

I wish that I had thought of something better
but instead I went home and cried
for all that could've been if we hadn't lost you.

Error

I'm in the emergency room
listening to a woman talk about her preferred brand of condoms
and the possible rash that (hopefully) isn't an std.

I'm staring at the floor tiles,
hoping that a ghost of a saint or other higher up
will deem me worthy of a little holy intervention and
stop the shit show that I know is coming.

I'm in the emergency room
at an hour that is neither night or day

listening to my grandpa sleep because this pain
has exhausted both of us and he's the only one with an option
of not being awake.

I'm having a panic attack
hoping that the table isn't too tall or too difficult to traverse
and I'm debating whether I can convince someone to change their mind
and save some of my dignity.

I'm in the emergency room
listening to a man watch some video on his phone
and at least one of us is laughing.

I'm seriously having a panic attack
screaming my head off while the nurse looks like
she wants to punch me in the face and honestly,
I wouldn't blame her.

I'm in the emergency room
staring at the ceiling tiles and hoping
I'll die from the embarrassment before
I have to live through one more day of pain.

Discontent

You never lie but
are more truthful
in your silence

I will Be

Let's not lie to each other
by omission
No, I'm not okay
I haven't been
holding up
or keeping it together
or taking care of myself

Between injury and apathy
It's a wonder that I
find the energy
to get out of bed in the ~~morning~~
~~afternoon~~ evening

Nadia Hasan

or remember to eat
or do anything except write
and try to purge myself
of all the horrible things
I've been feeling

My mind doesn't rest
ever

Healing is exhausting
and unglamorous
but I do the best I can
every day
and some days are better than others

I won't make you promises I can't keep
but bear with me
I've never been the best
at getting better
but I always find a way through

How are you?

As for me,
I'm not okay
but
I will be

There Will Be A Day

Nothing lasts forever
not even this
no matter how bad it gets
I will stay with you

I will love you through the worst of it
and no matter what you think
there will be a day
that it all gets better
there will be a day
when you will find peace

whenever

(For my siblings, but especially my youngest sister)

Because of the love I was shown
I now understand how to best love you
I'm prepared
Whatever words you fashion out of
your anger and anguish,
I recognize the signs
and I wish I could tell you that
my love for you is a well that will never run dry

My best friend used to say,
"embrace your powerhouse-ness!"
but I couldn't see what she saw,

Nadia Hasan

I declared:
"I'm not a powerhouse
I'm just…
a lighthouse."

Let me be that for you

Let me be the one thing you can always find
when it gets too dark

Count on me
to be there, to stay
to keep you from crashing
on life's jagged edges

No matter how far you try
to push me away
I will stand firm,

my light and my love
never too far
to reach you

ACKNOWLEDGEMENTS

This book wouldn't exist without the love and support of so many people. If I forget you, please know that I still love and appreciate you.

A million special thanks to the wonderful team that made this book possible: Najla Qamber for her breathtaking cover design, Dionne Lister for her fantastic editing and Nadège Richards for her wonderful formatting!

To Papa, who never ceases to believe that I'll be the one-in-a-million kind of famous someday. Thank you for putting up with me, my late nights/early morning, all my "weird" tendencies and for loving me through everything. I love you, and I appreciate everything you do, even when I don't show it. To Mom, for allowing me to be open and honest on the page, even when it hurts you. To Aunt Kelly, who teaches me that no matter what the circumstance or how high the odds might seem stacked against you, there is always a way through and a chance to begin again. To my entire family, thank you for your love and support. I wouldn't be who I am without the memories and experiences that you've contributed to my life.

Ashley, you've always been there to help me when I needed someone. You've loved me when I was at my worst and supported me when I was at my weakest. Thank you. Ginger, thank you for twenty-five years of friendship! Thank you for loving my work and for keeping me grounded when I get carried away. Elyse, I know things between us aren't always perfect and that we've had some difficult times but I will always admire your drive, ambition and creativity. I love you and I appreciate what you've brought into my life. Ashley F. (Phillip-Ashley), we haven't known each other for long, but I felt it was important to say thank you for being there when the world fell apart. Thank you for being here still. Eli, you shouldn't be surprised that you're included in here. Thank you, for every reason that I've told you before and for all the help you've given to me and my work.

To Colleen Gleason, one of the best authors I know. Thank you. I am beyond blessed to know you and call you an "unofficial" mentor. I have learned so much from you, and I hope that I put it to good use going forward. I hope I can make you proud. To Ben Ditmars, the first person to call me a poet. Your work inspires me. Thank you for your friendship and for Inhale The Night. To Amber Jerome-Norrgard for your poetry and for believing in my own. To Dionne Lister, for encouraging me in more ways than one. To the both of you, for TweepNation.

Lastly, thank you, dear reader, for giving this book a chance. I hope that you find something in it to love.

ABOUT NADIA

Nadia Hasan is a writer and poet living in Detroit, MI. Following wherever the path of inspiration leads, she strives to cultivate hope, awareness and empathy through her writing. Her work has appeared in The Mirror News under their "Through the Looking Glass" segment, The Michigan Ave. Creative Arts Journal, and Rewriting Mary Sue. She also writes paranormal fiction as N.J. Ember. Visit her website: http://www.nadiajwriter.com/

www.ingramcontent.com/pod-product-compliance
Lightning Source LLC
Chambersburg PA
CBHW071746080526
44588CB00013B/2168